Breadcrumbs and Sunflower Seeds

Christopher Kim

Presentation by *BookLeaf Publishing*

Web: www.bookleafpub.com

E-mail: info@bookleafpub.com

ISBN: 9789357213738

First edition 2023

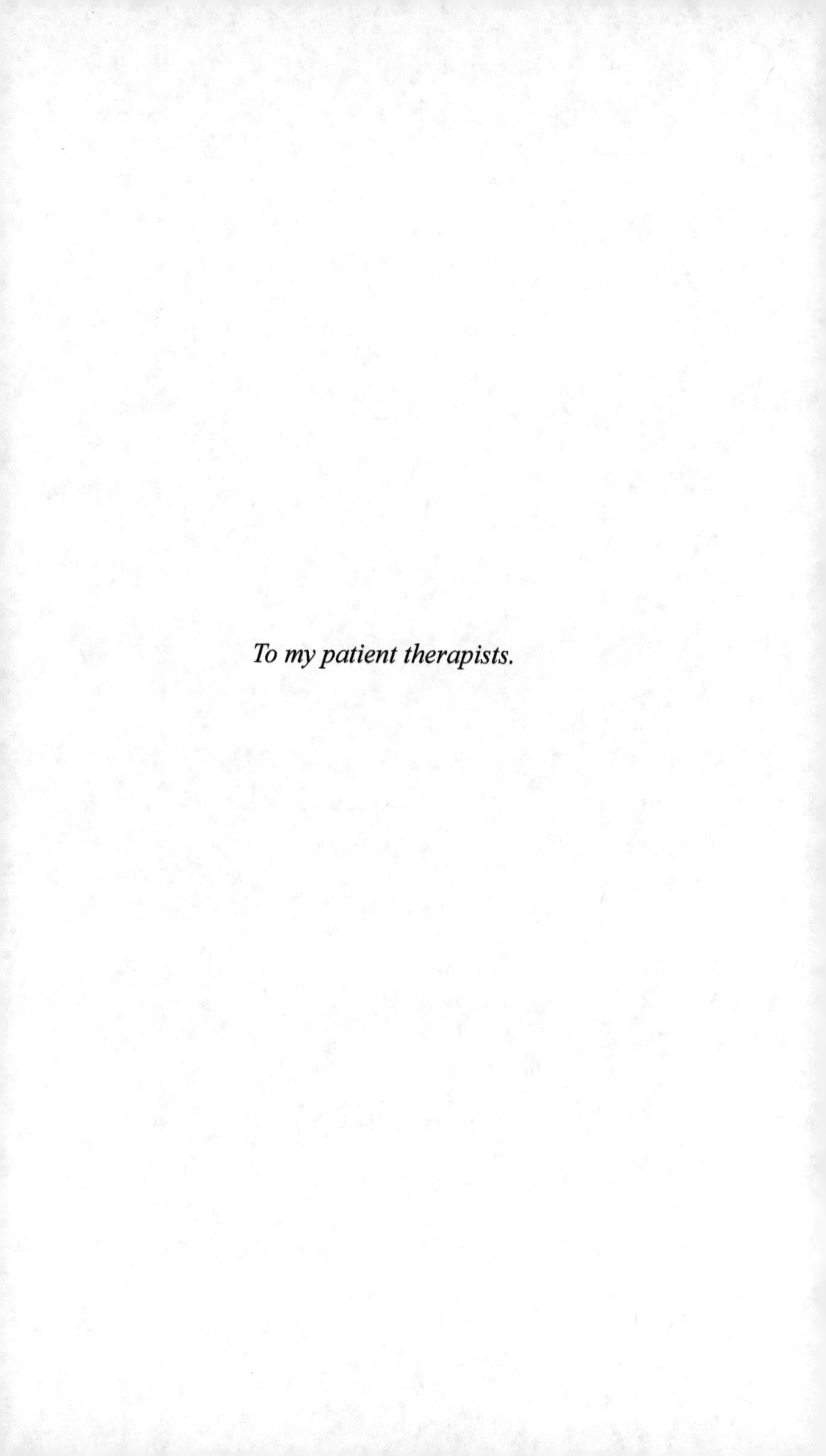

To my patient therapists.

ACKNOWLEDGEMENT

Thank you.

PREFACE

These poems help me cope with real world issues, like racism, chronic depression, and cat litter polluting the earth.

Volley

worst off
than Warsaw
in the Second World War
that we saw
watch the powers play
on the seesaw
no one move.
it's martial law.
run for the door
they made the call
hide your kids
don't withdraw
try to breath
airway's caught off.
thick thugs
behind a thin wall
hands up
bodies fall
missing autopsy
cameras uninstalled
paid leave
blue unions never stall
watch the powers play
on the seesaw

In the Middle

How do we compromise
Without compromising our integrity?
Why isn't the threshold for abuse at zero?

Whenever there's a discussion about rape,
It's no longer about who gets hurt,
It's about how many.

Somehow the numbers steal the limelight,
While the emotions get gaslit by a White knight.
"What are the odds?"

The consequences of the suspect
Are front page news.
A survivor's trauma gets far less views.

If the subject changes to race hate,
Everything becomes coincidental.
Speak nicely or else you're judgmental.

Is it possible that the wrong people
Continue to have a platform?
Can we stop enabling their bad form?

Let's start with the naïve optimists
Because they insist that problems
Are not that atrocious.

Deport the willfully ignorant.
Cast them out of their middle fortress.
Expose them to the classless.

But

Not to brag but,

I'm not racist but,

Not to be rude but,

I'm not sexist but,

Not to be offensive but,

I'm not a therapist but,

Not to sound judgmental but,

I'm not saying you're wrong but,

Welcome to the Meat Grinder

Home of the brave and expendable
Donate your blood to the top 1%
Watch as they paint the fields
With the Devil's paintbrush
It's a stroke of baneful genius

It only took one machinist
To produce an endless stream
Of fruitless promises
Only to yield a trough
Of cannon fodder

Cry for the naïve martyr
Share the story
Perpetuate the complex cycle
This modern industry
Needs more soldiers

The Black Dog

From the bottom of the stairs
Stares up at his desire
Nothing else compares

He cries and moans
Unrequited lust
Breaks his bones

But she's scared
Frozen stiff
Soul still not repaired

They lock eyes
Telepathic queries
Feelings in disguise

From the bottom of the stares
Good intentions
Mixed with bad visions

Like oil and water
Emulsive affairs

Wide Asleep

From dusk til dawn
Rationalizing yesterday
Speculating tomorrow

A lifetime of captive apes
Paralyzes my brainstem

Polluted rivers
Drown my chest

Dazed vines
Entangle my spine

As I lie at night
Reliving my sins
Planning my demise

Fuck Me

Only 15 more
Of this abomination
Stupid distraction
For my addiction
Can't quit now
This is my vacation
Financial modesty
Intellectual self-penetration
Cue the lights
Looking for salvation
Lost in decay
Wishing for commiseration

They

Assign us
To remind us
That they want
To restrain us

Live like their boy
Obey like their girls
Serve like their women
Die like their men

Circumcise
Rinse
Bleed
Repeat

Mint Condition

Pedigree Gold!
No creases, no stress lines, no stains.
Each corner is intact and perfectly 90 degrees.
All the pages are there;
Including the value stamp and ads.
The spine is smooth.
The edges are sharp.
Colors are still bright
And the white borders are still pure.
I'll be the last to experience this
High quality book
Before I lock it away in its plastic case.
Forever preserved.
Forever untouched.
Forever.

Leaky Faucet

Each drip echoes
Down the hallway
Reminding me
Of unfinished business
And wasted chances
I'm alone
In my apartment
Hearing
The weight of the drop
Desperately cling to the faucet
Before the full force of gravity
Pulls it down
Smacking onto the stainless steel

Plop

I listen
But, I can't be bothered
To fix it

I'm Old Testament

Give me your bold
And I will humble them
Bring me your deceitful
And I will reform them

The cost of purity is high
And the world is filthy
Nothing goes unjudged
Every sin needs cleansing

The mission for purification
Does not rest

Endless sacrifice
For an endless fight

Righteous life
Righteous death

Black and white
Right and wrong

Breadcrumbs and Sunflower Seeds

A man sits under the gazebo on a summer
afternoon
Beads of sweat run down the glass of iced tea
As the crumbs of the last bite of a tomato
sandwich
Sprinkle over the oak top
Shells from sunflower seeds get kicked under
the table

The maid rushes up the steps with a broom and
pan
Her lean and agile figure allow her to clean the
shells
Like an invisible ballerina
He politely shifts his plump feet to help clear the
way
Everything looks perfect on this beautiful
Sunday

The workers move in synchrony
As the wind breezes through the fields
And the golden rays prance across the land
All is well on Smith's plantation
Even the dogs rest with no protest
Everything looks perfect

Hotdogs

Delicious hotdogs
So many ways to enjoy
Hotdogs

Slap them on a bun
Fry them with rice
Mix them with eggs
Grill them
Dunk them in batter
Stuff them in a pretzel
Fill them with cheese
Wrap them in bacon
Throw them in grease

Share them at the school
Share them at the work
Share them at the home
Share them at the hospital
Share them at the prison
Share them at the shelter

Just please enjoy the hotdogs

The Good Neighbor

Here I am practicing sounding benign
At six in the morning in front of my mirror.

I call out sick.

I finish my tea and choke down my vitamins.

My neighbor and I move our trash cans back in
at the same time, so we wave at each other.

There's no more poop bags for my dog, so I
have to use a Zip-Loc bag.

 I schedule a pizza order 5 hours in advance.

I grab my bottle of whiskey and sit in front of
my laptop.

I drink and I stream.

The doorbell rings. It's the pizza.

I high five the delivery person and waddle back
to my show.

...

Here I am practicing sounding benign.

Chasing Rabbits

There's a place where we used to chase rabbits.
We went there after school during the spring.
It was too hot in the summer, too cold in the
winter,
and too misty in the fall.

We ran down the hill, hoping that the rabbits
would trip,
Instead, one of us would tumble and fall.

In the field at the bottom of the hill,
We ran like wild demons.
The rabbits cut left, cut right, circled us,
And always beat us.

Now the fields are filled with condos.
There's no more room to run.
No more rabbits to chase.

Hey Aliens

Please, give us a chance!
I promise that we will be nice.
It may not always look inviting, but Earth is
pretty cool.
We have frogs that jump high,
cheetahs that run fast,
plants that eat bugs,
and cows that make milk.

There are also sweet drinks that tickle your nose,
candy that makes your face implode,
and cheese that smells like fart.

Please ignore the re-education camps,
detention centers, and not so secret torture
chambers.

The nuclear waste problem is being resolved and
we have our smartest people repairing the ozone
layer.

Some of the water is still safe to drink and
the air is pretty good most of the time.

Don't let the guns and bombs scare you. We
probably won't
use them.

So, when you get a chance, please stop by.
Thanks.

Not Last

Maryland may not be the first in everything, but

it's also not the last.

It's not the first state to allow gay marriage.

legalize weed

ban child marriage

grant women the right to vote

repeal the ban on interracial marriage

end segregation in school

decriminalize abortion

recognize civil unions

mandate the use of seat belts

require Covid vaccination

and finally

It's also not the first state to prohibit cat declawing.

But, it's also not the last.

Goodnight

It's been a long day.
The mandatory social engagements
robbed me of my energy.
I am a depleted battery.
There's no more juice left.
I lie face down on the couch
with half my body hanging off the edge,
while half my mind is floating off to space.
There's no use for caffeine now.
It's only going to irritate my mood
and my bowels.
I wish there was someone here
to hook me up to an IV drip.
Or put a bullet in the back of my head.
Or feed me ice cream.
I don't know.
I'm tired.
I'm tired of experiencing.
Let me be.
I was not programmed for this.
I can feel it in my bones,
cartilage, organs, blood, nails, hair,
and liver bile.
Every molecule in my body is screaming:

AHHHHH TURN IT ALL OFF AHHHH

End of rant. Goodnight.